The Teachable Moment
An Educator's Workbook

Matthew Goodall

Copyright © 2023 by Matthew Goodall.

No part of this book may be used or reproduced in any form on or by any electronic or mechanical means, including information storage and retrieval systems, without permission in writing from the publisher, except by a reviewer who may quote brief passages in a review.

All rights reserved.

Due to the dynamic nature of the Internet, any web addresses or links contained in this book may have changed since publication and may no longer be valid. The views expressed in this work are solely those of the author and do not necessarily reflect the views of the publisher, and the publisher hereby disclaims any responsibility for them.

This publication is designed to provide accurate and authoritative information in regard to the subject matter covered. It is sold with the understanding that neither the author nor the publisher is engaged in rendering legal, investment, accounting or other professional services. While the publisher and author have used their best efforts in preparing this book, they make no representations or warranties with respect to the accuracy or completeness of the contents of this book and specifically disclaim any implied warranties of merchantability or fitness for a particular purpose. No warranty may be created or extended by sales representatives or written sales materials. The advice and strategies contained herein may not be suitable for your situation. You should consult with a professional when appropriate. Neither the publisher nor the author shall be liable for any loss of profit or any other commercial damages, including but not limited to special, incidental, consequential, personal, or other damages.

Book Cover by MidJourney.

Illustrations by MidJourney, and Matthew Goodall.

Book design by Matthew Goodall

ISBN: 978-1-7386047-2-2 (Print)

ISBN: 978-1-7386047-3-9 (E-book)

Published by Matthew Goodall (Aotearoa / New Zealand).

www.matthewgoodall.org

Contents

1. Introduction	1
What is the Teachable Moment?	
1: Colours	4
1: Numbers	6
1: Shapes	8
1: Alphabet	12
1: Animals	16
1: Imaginative Play	18
2: Colours	20
2: Numbers	22
2: Shapes	24
2: Alphabet	28
2: Animals	32
2: Imaginative Play	34
3: Colours	36
3: Numbers	38
3: Shapes	40
3: Alphabet	44

3: Animals	48
3: Imaginative Play	50
4: Colours	52
4: Numbers	54
4: Shapes	56
4: Alphabet	60
4: Animals	64
4: Imaginative Play	66
5: Colours	68
5: Numbers	70
5: Shapes	72
5: Alphabet	76
5: Animals	80
5: Imaginative Play	82
6: Colours	84
6: Numbers	86
6: Shapes	88
6: Alphabet	92
6: Animals	96
6: Imaginative Play	98
7: Colours	100
7: Numbers	102
7: Shapes	104

7: Alphabet	108
7: Animals	112
7: Imaginative Play	114
8: Colours	116
8: Numbers	118
8: Shapes	120
8: Alphabet	124
8: Animals	128
8: Imaginative Play	130
9: Colours	132
9: Numbers	134
9: Shapes	136
9: Alphabet	140
9: Animals	144
9: Imaginative Play	146
10: Colours	148
10: Numbers	150
10: Shapes	152
10: Alphabet	156
10: Animals	160
10: Imaginative Play	162
Also By Matthew Goodall	164
About the Author	165

Chapter 166

Introduction

What is the Teachable Moment?

The Miriam Webster online dictionary defines the teachable moment as: 'a time that is favorable for teaching something...'

(https://www.merriam-webster.com/dictionary/teachable%20moment - 24/02/2023)

It's that subtle point in time when you are able to point someone, young or old, in the direction of new knowledge because they're open to it.

Wikipedia defines it as: 'the time at which learning a particular topic or idea becomes possible or easiest.'

(https://en.wikipedia.org/wiki/Teachable_moment - 25/02/2023)

The Teachable Moment is all about knowing the child and their capacity for extra extension, as well as what they are interested in.

"Be intentional and look for teachable moments." (Marybeth Hicks, Teachable Moments, published by Howard Books, 2015).

Every concept that a child learns can be linked into another, so that you can extend on their learning, right in the moment that they're engaged with you.

You might be talking about the shape of a window: you can ask what letter 'window' starts with; what colour it is; what shape etc.

If your child prefers to 'do' instead of just talking (hands-on learning), you can encourage them to draw or make the thing with blocks, play dough and so on.

Each of the resources in the following pages has been designed to be as simple as possible, not because I think that adults don't know simple things like colours, but because life is full of many complicated things that we have to keep track of, and sometimes it's the 'little' things that slip our minds.

It isn't a comprehensive list, but is just a starting point to help you support the children in your life.

The pages are repeated 10 times, and grouped together so you can use them for each child individually.

If you want more copies of individual pages you can download these at: https://www.matthewgoodall.org/ttmresources

**The Teachable Moment: An Educator's Resource (ISBN: 978-1-7386047-0-8), is available to order through your usual retailers,
or as an E-Book (ISBN: 978-1-7386047-1-5).**

1: Colours

What is your child's favourite colour? _____

Primary colours are red, blue, and yellow.

Secondary colours are purple, green, and orange.

Red + blue = purple.

Blue + yellow = green.

Yellow + red = orange.

Red + white = pink.

Black is no colour.

White is all colours – *if you have a prism or a crystal you can show how the light breaks up into a rainbow.*

Black + white = grey.

Rainbow colours, in order: Red; Orange; Yellow; Green; Blue; Indigo; Violet

What letter does THEIR FAVOURITE COLOUR _____ start with?

What other things start with that letter?

How many things can you see that start with (the first letter of the favourite colour)?

What COLOUR _____ things do you like to eat?

(If the favourite colour is a **primary colour**):
What colour do you get if you mix
THEIR FAVOURITE COLOUR _____ and ANOTHER COLOUR?

(If the favourite colour is a **secondary colour**):
What colours do you mix to make THEIR FAVOURITE COLOUR _____ ?

Can you think of any songs about THEIR FAVOURITE COLOUR _____ ?

Encourage them to draw things in THEIR FAVOURITE COLOUR.

1: Numbers

For young children, counting should be a reasonably simple task, starting with very basic and working their way up.

How many tummies do you have? *(The answer is one, even if they do seem to eat like they have 2!)*

How many necks?

How many backs?

How many hands do you have?

How many legs / eyes / ears etc?

How many thumbs?

How many fingers? *(It's up to you if you count thumbs along with the fingers)*

This is where you can start to show how different groups can still make the same number (eg. 2 fingers + 2 fingers, or, 3 fingers + 1 finger, or, 4 fingers - all add up to 4).

A song like BINGO is good for learning about the sequence, clapping as each letter of the name is replaced.

There are numerous other songs about counting (I'm *not* thinking of '99 bottles of pop on the wall'!) You can find many examples online to sing along with.

If your child is interested in animals, count how many eyes, legs, different colours etc. they have.

Older children may be able to start to discuss the letters that numbers start with (One is 'o' - even though it sounds like a 'w'; Two is 't' etc).

You can encourage children to draw or write the numbers, draw groups of objects (eg. cars, animals), that have a specific number - one car, two dogs etc.

They may prefer to count physical objects - how many toy cars, how many books, how many cookies (and then you can talk about how many things have been subtracted!)

1: Shapes

Knowing which shapes your child might be interested in can help you be on the look out for them in everyday life.

If they particularly like physical play you can encourage them to make, build or draw different shapes.

Here are a few examples.

- **Circles:**
- Eyes
- Your hand/s can make small and big circle shapes
- Pot plant containers

- Wheels.

- **Squares:**

  - Windows
  - Dice
  - Chocolate squares
  - Cakes

- **Rectangles:**

  - Doors
  - Microwaves
  - Windows
  - Books

- **Triangles:**

  - Pizza slice
  - Pyramid
  - Your hands can make triangle shapes
  - The roof of a house

- **Ovals:**

  - Eggs

  - Football

  - Some mirrors

  - Avocado

- **Hexagons (6 sides):**

  - Honeycomb / Bee hive

  - Bolt

  - Floor tiles

  - The pattern on a soccer ball

- **Octagons (8 sides):**

  - Stop sign

  - Floor tiles

  - Jewellery

  - Clock face

1: Alphabet

Children often love to sing the alphabet song, and this can be a crucial part of learning.

Ways to extend on it can be to ask, "What can you think of that starts with 'A'?" etc.

Ask them to draw. If they suggest an animal you can talk about the sounds they make, or pretend to be one (eg. a rabbit hopping).

Here are a few suggestions of each letter to help get you started:

A: Apple; Aeroplane; Ant

B: Ball; Baby; Blue

C: Cat; Car; Caravan

D: Dog; Duck; Doll

E: Elephant; Egg; Eye

F: Fish; Frog; Fairy

G: Goat; Ghost; Gold

H: Hippopotamus; Hair; Home

I: Ice Cream; Igloo; Iris (coloured part of the eye)

J: Jump; Jeans; Jelly

K: Kangaroo; Koala; Key

L: Love; Lion; Light

M: Man; Moon; Mouse

N: Necklace; Noodles; Newspaper

O: Orange; Opossum; Oven

P: Purple; Princess; Party

Q: Queen; Quail; Quilt

R: Rabbit; Rainbow; Robot

S: Sun; Spaghetti; Soccer

T: Tree; Tiger; Train

U: Umbrella; Unicorn; Ukelele

V: Violin; Volcano; Vegetables

W: Whale; Water; Walrus

X: Xylophone; X-ray; Xenopus (a type of frog)

Y: Yellow; Yoga; Yacht

Z: Zebra; Zucchini; Zip

1: Animals

What colour is it?

What letter does it start with?

How many legs does it have?

What colour / colours is it?

What does it eat?

What letter does that food start with?

Encourage them to draw the animal – in real colours and imaginative ones.

What songs might include this animal?

1: Imaginative Play

Children love to play, and love to play pretend.

Whether they are in the sandpit, climbing trees, building pillow and blanket forts or playing with blocks, there are so many ways to drop in a quick little moment of learning.

The following are only a set of starters to prompt you.

- **In the sandpit:**
  - What colour is the sand?
  - What letter does that start with?
  - How does it feel?

- **Climbing trees:**

- What colour is the tree? leaves?

- What letter does that start with?

- Can you see anything hiding in the tree? (insects, birds etc).

- **Building forts:**

- How many pillows have you used?

- What shape are they?

- What colours are they?

- **Blocks:**

- What are you building?

- What letter does that start with?

- How many blocks have you used?

2: Colours

What is your child's favourite colour? _____

Primary colours are red, blue, and yellow.

Secondary colours are purple, green, and orange.

Red + blue = purple.

Blue + yellow = green.

Yellow + red = orange.

Red + white = pink.

Black is no colour.

White is all colours – *if you have a prism or a crystal you can show how the light breaks up into a rainbow.*

Black + white = grey.

Rainbow colours, in order: Red; Orange; Yellow; Green; Blue; Indigo; Violet

What letter does THEIR FAVOURITE COLOUR _____ start with?

What other things start with that letter?

How many things can you see that start with (the first letter of the favourite colour)?

What COLOUR _____ things do you like to eat?

(If the favourite colour is a **primary colour**): What colour do you get if you mix THEIR FAVOURITE COLOUR _____ and ANOTHER COLOUR?

(If the favourite colour is a **secondary colour**): What colours do you mix to make THEIR FAVOURITE COLOUR _____ ?

Can you think of any songs about THEIR FAVOURITE COLOUR _____ ?

Encourage them to draw things in THEIR FAVOURITE COLOUR.

2: Numbers

For young children, counting should be a reasonably simple task, starting with very basic and working their way up.

How many tummies do you have? *(The answer is one, even if they do seem to eat like they have 2!)*

How many necks?

How many backs?

How many hands do you have?

How many legs / eyes / ears etc?

How many thumbs?

How many fingers? *(It's up to you if you count thumbs along with the fingers)*

This is where you can start to show how different groups can still make the same number (eg. 2 fingers + 2 fingers, or, 3 fingers + 1 finger, or, 4 fingers – all add up to 4).

A song like BINGO is good for learning about the sequence, clapping as each letter of the name is replaced.

There are numerous other songs about counting (I'm *not* thinking of '99 bottles of pop on the wall'!) You can find many examples online to sing along with.

If your child is interested in animals, count how many eyes, legs, different colours etc. they have.

Older children may be able to start to discuss the letters that numbers start with (One is 'o' – even though it sounds like a 'w'; Two is 't' etc).

You can encourage children to draw or write the numbers, draw groups of objects (eg. cars, animals), that have a specific number – one car, two dogs etc.

They may prefer to count physical objects – how many toy cars, how many books, how many cookies (and then you can talk about how many things have been subtracted!)

2: Shapes

Knowing which shapes your child might be interested in can help you be on the look out for them in everyday life.

If they particularly like physical play you can encourage them to make, build or draw different shapes.

Here are a few examples.

- **Circles:**
- Eyes
- Your hand/s can make small and big circle shapes
- Pot plant containers

- Wheels.

- **Squares:**

- Windows

- Dice

- Chocolate squares

- Cakes

- **Rectangles:**

- Doors

- Microwaves

- Windows

- Books

- **Triangles:**

- Pizza slice

- Pyramid

- Your hands can make triangle shapes

- The roof of a house

- **Ovals:**

  - Eggs

  - Football

  - Some mirrors

  - Avocado

- **Hexagons (6 sides):**

  - Honeycomb / Bee hive

  - Bolt

  - Floor tiles

  - The pattern on a soccer ball

- **Octagons (8 sides):**

  - Stop sign

  - Floor tiles

  - Jewellery

  - Clock face

2: Alphabet

Children often love to sing the alphabet song, and this can be a crucial part of learning.

Ways to extend on it can be to ask, "What can you think of that starts with 'A'?" etc.

Ask them to draw. If they suggest an animal you can talk about the sounds they make, or pretend to be one (eg. a rabbit hopping).

Here are a few suggestions to help get you started:

A: Apple; Aeroplane; Ant

B: Ball; Baby; Blue

C: Cat; Car; Caravan

D: Dog; Duck; Doll

E: Elephant; Egg; Eye

F: Fish; Frog; Fairy

G: Goat; Ghost; Gold

H: Hippopotamus; Hair; Home

I: Ice Cream; Igloo; Iris (coloured part of the eye)

J: Jump; Jeans; Jelly

K: Kangaroo; Koala; Key

L: Love; Lion; Light

M: Man; Moon; Mouse

N: Necklace; Noodles; Newspaper

O: Orange; Opossum; Oven

P: Purple; Princess; Party

Q: Queen; Quail; Quilt

R: Rabbit; Rainbow; Robot

S: Sun; Spaghetti; Soccer

T: Tree; Tiger; Train

U: Umbrella; Unicorn; Ukelele

V: Violin; Volcano; Vegetables

W: Whale; Water; Walrus

X: Xylophone; X-ray; Xenopus (a type of frog)

Y: Yellow; Yoga; Yacht

Z: Zebra; Zucchini; Zip

2: Animals

What colour is it?

What letter does it start with?

How many legs does it have?

What colour / colours is it?

What does it eat?

What letter does that food start with?

Encourage them to draw the animal – in real colours and imaginative ones.

What songs might include this animal?

2: Imaginative Play

Children love to play, and love to play pretend.

Whether they are in the sandpit, climbing trees, building pillow and blanket forts or playing with Lego, there are so many ways to drop in a quick little moment of learning.

The following are only a set of starters to prompt you.

- **In the sandpit:**

  - What colour is the sand?

  - What letter does that start with?

  - How does it feel?

- **Climbing trees:**

- What colour is the tree? leaves?

- What letter does that start with?

- Can you see anything hiding in the tree? (insects, birds etc).

- **Building forts:**

- How many pillows have you used?

- What shape are they?

- What colours are they?

- **Lego:**

- What are you building?

- What letter does that start with?

- How many blocks have you used?

3: Colours

What is your child's favourite colour? _____

Primary colours are red, blue, and yellow.

Secondary colours are purple, green, and orange.

Red + blue = purple.

Blue + yellow = green.

Yellow + red = orange.

Red + white = pink.

Black is no colour.

White is all colours – *if you have a prism or a crystal you can show how the light breaks up into a rainbow.*

Black + white = grey.

Rainbow colours, in order: Red; Orange; Yellow; Green; Blue; Indigo; Violet

What letter does THEIR FAVOURITE COLOUR _____ start with?

What other things start with that letter?

How many things can you see that start with (the first letter of the favourite colour)?

What COLOUR _____ things do you like to eat?

(If the favourite colour is a **primary colour**): What colour do you get if you mix THEIR FAVOURITE COLOUR _____ and ANOTHER COLOUR?

(If the favourite colour is a **secondary colour**): What colours do you mix to make THEIR FAVOURITE COLOUR _____ ?

Can you think of any songs about THEIR FAVOURITE COLOUR _____ ?

Encourage them to draw things in THEIR FAVOURITE COLOUR.

3: Numbers

For young children, counting should be a reasonably simple task, starting with very basic and working their way up.

How many tummies do you have? *(The answer is one, even if they do seem to eat like they have 2!)*

How many necks?

How many backs?

How many hands do you have?

How many legs / eyes / ears etc?

How many thumbs?

How many fingers? *(It's up to you if you count thumbs along with the fingers)*

This is where you can start to show how different groups can still make the same number (eg. 2 fingers + 2 fingers, or, 3 fingers + 1 finger, or, 4 fingers – all add up to 4).

A song like BINGO is good for learning about the sequence, clapping as each letter of the name is replaced.

There are numerous other songs about counting (I'm *not* thinking of '99 bottles of pop on the wall'!) You can find many examples online to sing along with.

If your child is interested in animals, count how many eyes, legs, different colours etc. they have.

Older children may be able to start to discuss the letters that numbers start with (One is 'o' – even though it sounds like a 'w'; Two is 't' etc).

You can encourage children to draw or write the numbers, draw groups of objects (eg. cars, animals), that have a specific number – one car, two dogs etc.

They may prefer to count physical objects – how many toy cars, how many books, how many cookies (and then you can talk about how many things have been subtracted!)

3: Shapes

Knowing which shapes your child might be interested in can help you be on the look out for them in everyday life.

If they particularly like physical play you can encourage them to make, build or draw different shapes.

Here are a few examples.

- **Circles:**
- Eyes
- Your hand/s can make small and big circle shapes
- Pot plant containers

- Wheels.

- **Squares:**

- Windows

- Dice

- Chocolate squares

- Cakes

- **Rectangles:**

- Doors

- Microwaves

- Windows

- Books

- **Triangles:**

- Pizza slice

- Pyramid

- Your hands can make triangle shapes

- The roof of a house

- **Ovals:**

  - Eggs

  - Football

  - Some mirrors

  - Avocado

- **Hexagons (6 sides):**

  - Honeycomb / Bee hive

  - Bolt

  - Floor tiles

  - The pattern on a soccer ball

- **Octagons (8 sides):**

  - Stop sign

  - Floor tiles

  - Jewellery

  - Clock face

3: Alphabet

Children often love to sing the alphabet song, and this can be a crucial part of learning.

Ways to extend on it can be to ask, "What can you think of that starts with 'A'?" etc.

Ask them to draw. If they suggest an animal you can talk about the sounds they make, or pretend to be one (eg. a rabbit hopping).

Here are a few suggestions to help get you started:

A: Apple; Aeroplane; Ant

B: Ball; Baby; Blue

C: Cat; Car; Caravan

D: Dog; Duck; Doll

E: Elephant; Egg; Eye

F: Fish; Frog; Fairy

G: Goat; Ghost; Gold

H: Hippopotamus; Hair; Home

I: Ice Cream; Igloo; Iris (coloured part of the eye)

J: Jump; Jeans; Jelly

K: Kangaroo; Koala; Key

L: Love; Lion; Light

M: Man; Moon; Mouse

N: Necklace; Noodles; Newspaper

O: Orange; Opossum; Oven

P: Purple; Princess; Party

Q: Queen; Quail; Quilt

R: Rabbit; Rainbow; Robot

S: Sun; Spaghetti; Soccer

T: Tree; Tiger; Train

U: Umbrella; Unicorn; Ukelele

V: Violin; Volcano; Vegetables

W: Whale; Water; Walrus

X: Xylophone; X-ray; Xenopus (a type of frog)

Y: Yellow; Yoga; Yacht

Z: Zebra; Zucchini; Zip

3: Animals

What colour is it?

What letter does it start with?

How many legs does it have?

What colour / colours is it?

What does it eat?

What letter does that food start with?

Encourage them to draw the animal – in real colours and imaginative ones.

What songs might include this animal?

3: Imaginative Play

Children love to play, and love to play pretend.

Whether they are in the sandpit, climbing trees, building pillow and blanket forts or playing with Lego, there are so many ways to drop in a quick little moment of learning.

The following are only a set of starters to prompt you.

- **In the sandpit:**

  - What colour is the sand?

  - What letter does that start with?

  - How does it feel?

- **Climbing trees:**

- What colour is the tree? leaves?

- What letter does that start with?

- Can you see anything hiding in the tree? (insects, birds etc).

- **Building forts:**

- How many pillows have you used?

- What shape are they?

- What colours are they?

- **Lego:**

- What are you building?

- What letter does that start with?

- How many blocks have you used?

4: Colours

What is your child's favourite colour? _____

Primary colours are red, blue, and yellow.

Secondary colours are purple, green, and orange.

Red + blue = purple.

Blue + yellow = green.

Yellow + red = orange.

Red + white = pink.

Black is no colour.

White is all colours – *if you have a prism or a crystal you can show how the light breaks up into a rainbow.*

Black + white = grey.

Rainbow colours, in order: Red; Orange; Yellow; Green; Blue; Indigo; Violet

What letter does THEIR FAVOURITE COLOUR _____ start with?

What other things start with that letter?

How many things can you see that start with (the first letter of the favourite colour)?

What COLOUR _____ things do you like to eat?

(If the favourite colour is a **primary colour**):
What colour do you get if you mix
THEIR FAVOURITE COLOUR _____ and ANOTHER COLOUR?

(If the favourite colour is a **secondary colour**):
What colours do you mix to make THEIR FAVOURITE COLOUR _____ ?

Can you think of any songs about THEIR FAVOURITE COLOUR _____ ?

Encourage them to draw things in THEIR FAVOURITE COLOUR.

4: Numbers

For young children, counting should be a reasonably simple task, starting with very basic and working their way up.

How many tummies do you have? *(The answer is one, even if they do seem to eat like they have 2!)*

How many necks?

How many backs?

How many hands do you have?

How many legs / eyes / ears etc?

How many thumbs?

How many fingers? *(It's up to you if you count thumbs along with the fingers)*

This is where you can start to show how different groups can still make the same number (eg. 2 fingers + 2 fingers, or, 3 fingers + 1 finger, or, 4 fingers – all add up to 4).

A song like BINGO is good for learning about the sequence, clapping as each letter of the name is replaced.

There are numerous other songs about counting (I'm *not* thinking of '99 bottles of pop on the wall'!) You can find many examples online to sing along with.

If your child is interested in animals, count how many eyes, legs, different colours etc. they have.

Older children may be able to start to discuss the letters that numbers start with (One is 'o' – even though it sounds like a 'w'; Two is 't' etc).

You can encourage children to draw or write the numbers, draw groups of objects (eg. cars, animals), that have a specific number – one car, two dogs etc.

They may prefer to count physical objects – how many toy cars, how many books, how many cookies (and then you can talk about how many things have been subtracted!)

4: Shapes

Knowing which shapes your child might be interested in can help you be on the look out for them in everyday life.

If they particularly like physical play you can encourage them to make, build or draw different shapes.

Here are a few examples.

- **Circles:**
- Eyes
- Your hand/s can make small and big circle shapes
- Pot plant containers

- Wheels.

- **Squares:**

- Windows

- Dice

- Chocolate squares

- Cakes

- **Rectangles:**

- Doors

- Microwaves

- Windows

- Books

- **Triangles:**

- Pizza sl ce

- Pyramid

- Your hands can make triangle shapes

- The roof of a house

- **Ovals:**

  - Eggs

  - Football

  - Some mirrors

  - Avocado

- **Hexagons (6 sides):**

  - Honeycomb / Bee hive

  - Bolt

  - Floor tiles

  - The pattern on a soccer ball

- **Octagons (8 sides):**

  - Stop sign

  - Floor tiles

  - Jewellery

  - Clock face

4: Alphabet

Children often love to sing the alphabet song, and this can be a crucial part of learning.

Ways to extend on it can be to ask, "What can you think of that starts with 'A'?" etc.

Ask them to draw. If they suggest an animal you can talk about the sounds they make, or pretend to be one (eg. a rabbit hopping).

Here are a few suggestions of each letter to help get you started:

A: Apple; Aeroplane; Ant

B: Ball; Baby; Blue

C: Cat; Car; Caravan

D: Dog; Duck; Doll

E: Elephant; Egg; Eye

F: Fish; Frog; Fairy

G: Goat; Ghost; Gold

H: Hippopotamus; Hair; Home

I: Ice Cream; Igloo; Iris (coloured part of the eye)

J: Jump; Jeans; Jelly

K: Kangaroo; Koala; Key

L: Love; Lion; Light

M: Man; Moon; Mouse

N: Necklace; Noodles; Newspaper

O: Orange; Opossum; Oven

P: Purple; Princess; Party

Q: Queen; Quail; Quilt

R: Rabbit; Rainbow; Robot

S: Sun; Spaghetti; Soccer

T: Tree; Tiger; Train

U: Umbrella; Unicorn; Ukelele

V: Violin; Volcano; Vegetables

W: Whale; Water; Walrus

X: Xylophone; X-ray; Xenopus (a type of frog)

Y: Yellow; Yoga; Yacht

Z: Zebra; Zucchini; Zip

4: Animals

What colour is it?

What letter does it start with?

How many legs does it have?

What colour / colours is it?

What does it eat?

What letter does that food start with?

Encourage them to draw the animal – in real colours and imaginative ones.

What songs might include this animal?

4: Imaginative Play

Children love to play, and love to play pretend.

Whether they are in the sandpit, climbing trees, building pillow and blanket forts or playing with blocks, there are so many ways to drop in a quick little moment of learning.

The following are only a set of starters to prompt you.

- **In the sandpit:**

  - What colour is the sand?

  - What letter does that start with?

  - How does it feel?

- **Climbing trees:**

  - What colour is the tree? leaves?

  - What letter does that start with?

  - Can you see anything hiding in the tree? (insects, birds etc).

- **Building forts:**

  - How many pillows have you used?

  - What shape are they?

  - What colours are they?

- **Blocks:**

  - What are you building?

  - What letter does that start with?

  - How many blocks have you used?

5: Colours

What is your child's favourite colour? _____

Primary colours are red, blue, and yellow.

Secondary colours are purple, green, and orange.

Red + blue = purple.

Blue + yellow = green.

Yellow + red = orange.

Red + white = pink.

Black is no colour.

White is all colours – *if you have a prism or a crystal you can show how the light breaks up into a rainbow.*

Black + white = grey.

Rainbow colours, in order: Red; Orange; Yellow; Green; Blue; Indigo; Violet

What letter does THEIR FAVOURITE COLOUR _____ start with?

What other things start with that letter?

How many things can you see that start with (the first letter of the favourite colour)?

What COLOUR _____ things do you like to eat?

(If the favourite colour is a **primary colour**):
What colour do you get if you mix
THEIR FAVOURITE COLOUR _____ and ANOTHER COLOUR?

(If the favourite colour is a **secondary colour**):
What colours do you mix to make THEIR FAVOURITE COLOUR _____ ?

Can you think of any songs about THEIR FAVOURITE COLOUR _____ ?

Encourage them to draw things in THEIR FAVOURITE COLOUR.

5: Numbers

For young children, counting should be a reasonably simple task, starting with very basic and working their way up.

How many tummies do you have? *(The answer is one, even if they do seem to eat like they have 2!)*

How many necks?

How many backs?

How many hands do you have?

How many legs / eyes / ears etc?

How many thumbs?

How many fingers? *(It's up to you if you count thumbs along with the fingers)*

This is where you can start to show how different groups can still make the same number (eg. 2 fingers + 2 fingers, or, 3 fingers + 1 finger, or, 4 fingers – all add up to 4).

A song like BINGO is good for learning about the sequence, clapping as each letter of the name is replaced.

There are numerous other songs about counting (I'm *not* thinking of '99 bottles of pop on the wall'!) You can find many examples online to sing along with.

If your child is interested in animals, count how many eyes, legs, different colours etc. they have.

Older children may be able to start to discuss the letters that numbers start with (One is 'o' – even though it sounds like a 'w'; Two is 't' etc).

You can encourage children to draw or write the numbers, draw groups of objects (eg. cars, animals), that have a specific number – one car, two dogs etc.

They may prefer to count physical objects – how many toy cars, how many books, how many cookies (and then you can talk about how many things have been subtracted!)

5: Shapes

Knowing which shapes your child might be interested in can help you be on the look out for them in everyday life.

If they particularly like physical play you can encourage them to make, build or draw different shapes.

Here are a few examples.

- **Circles:**
- Eyes
- Your hand/s can make small and big circle shapes
- Pot plant containers

- Wheels.

- **Squares:**

  - Windows

  - Dice

  - Chocolate squares

  - Cakes

- **Rectangles:**

  - Doors

  - Microwaves

  - Windows

  - Books

- **Triangles:**

  - Pizza slice

  - Pyramid

  - Your hands can make triangle shapes

  - The roof of a house

- **Ovals:**

  - Eggs

  - Football

  - Some mirrors

  - Avocado

- **Hexagons (6 sides):**

  - Honeycomb / Bee hive

  - Bolt

  - Floor tiles

  - The pattern on a soccer ball

- **Octagons (8 sides):**

  - Stop sign

  - Floor tiles

  - Jewellery

  - Clock face

5: Alphabet

Children often love to sing the alphabet song, and this can be a crucial part of learning.

Ways to extend on it can be to ask, "What can you think of that starts with 'A'?" etc.

Ask them to draw. If they suggest an animal you can talk about the sounds they make, or pretend to be one (eg. a rabbit hopping).

Here are a few suggestions of each letter to help get you started:

A: Apple; Aeroplane; Ant

B: Ball; Baby; Blue

C: Cat; Car; Caravan

D: Dog; Duck; Doll

E: Elephant; Egg; Eye

F: Fish; Frog; Fairy

G: Goat; Ghost; Gold

H: Hippopotamus; Fair; Home

I: Ice Cream; Igloo; Iris (coloured part of the eye)

J: Jump; Jeans; Jelly

K: Kangaroo; Koala; Key

L: Love; Lion; Light

M: Man; Moon; Mouse

N: Necklace; Noodles; Newspaper

O: Orange; Opossum; Oven

P: Purple; Princess; Party

Q: Queen; Quail; Quilt

R: Rabbit; Rainbow; Robot

S: Sun; Spaghetti; Soccer

T: Tree; Tiger; Train

U: Umbrella; Unicorn; Ukelele

V: Violin; Volcano; Vegetables

W: Whale; Water; Walrus

X: Xylophone; X-ray; Xenopus (a type of frog)

Y: Yellow; Yoga; Yacht

Z: Zebra; Zucchini; Zip

5: Animals

What colour is it?

What letter does it start with?

How many legs does it have?

What colour / colours is it?

What does it eat?

What letter does that food start with?

Encourage them to draw the animal – in real colours and imaginative ones.

What songs might include this animal?

5: Imaginative Play

Children love to play, and love to play pretend.

Whether they are in the sandpit, climbing trees, building pillow and blanket forts or playing with blocks, there are so many ways to drop in a quick little moment of learning.

The following are only a set of starters to prompt you.

- **In the sandpit:**

  - What colour is the sand?

  - What letter does that start with?

  - How does it feel?

- **Climbing trees:**

  - What co our is the tree? leaves?

  - What letter does that start with?

  - Can you see anything hiding in the tree? (insects, birds etc).

- **Building forts:**

  - How many pillows have you used?

  - What shape are they?

  - What colours are they?

- **Blocks:**

  - What are you building?

  - What letter does that start with?

  - How many blocks have you used?

6: Colours

What is your child's favourite colour? _____

Primary colours are red, blue, and yellow.

Secondary colours are purple, green, and orange.

Red + blue = purple.

Blue + yellow = green.

Yellow + red = orange.

Red + white = pink.

Black is no colour.

White is all colours – *if you have a prism or a crystal you can show how the light breaks up into a rainbow.*

Black + white = grey.

Rainbow colours, in order: Red; Orange; Yellow; Green; Blue; Indigo; Violet

What letter does THEIR FAVOURITE COLOUR _____ start with?

What other things start with that letter?

How many things can you see that start with (the first letter of the favourite colour)?

What COLOUR _____ things do you like to eat?

(If the favourite colour is a **primary colour**):
What colour do you get if you mix
THEIR FAVOURITE COLOUR _____ and ANOTHER COLOUR?

(If the favourite colour is a **secondary colour**):
What colours do you mix to make THEIR FAVOURITE COLOUR _____ ?

Can you think of any songs about THEIR FAVOURITE COLOUR _____ ?

Encourage them to draw things in THEIR FAVOURITE COLOUR.

6: Numbers

For young children, counting should be a reasonably simple task, starting with very basic and working their way up.

How many tummies do you have? *(The answer is one, even if they do seem to eat like they have 2!)*

How many necks?

How many backs?

How many hands do you have?

How many legs / eyes / ears etc?

How many thumbs?

How many fingers? *(It's up to you if you count thumbs along with the fingers,*

This is where you can start to show how different groups can still make the same number (eg. 2 fingers + 2 fingers, or, 3 fingers + 1 finger, or, 4 fingers – all add up to 4).

A song like BINGO is good for learning about the sequence, clapping as each letter of the name is replaced.

There are numerous other songs about counting (I'm *not* thinking of '99 bottles of pop on the wall'!) You can find many examples online to sing along with.

If your child is interested in animals, count how many eyes, legs, different colours etc. they have.

Older children may be able to start to discuss the letters that numbers start with (One is 'o' – even though it sounds like a 'w'; Two is 't' etc).

You can encourage children to draw or write the numbers, draw groups of objects (eg. cars, animals), that have a specific number – one car, two dogs etc.

They may prefer to count physical objects – how many toy cars, how many books, how many cookies (and then you can talk about how many things have been subtracted!)

6: Shapes

Knowing which shapes your child might be interested in can help you be on the look out for them in everyday life.

If they particularly like physical play you can encourage them to make, build or draw different shapes.

Here are a few examples.

- **Circles:**
- Eyes
- Your hand/s can make small and big circle shapes
- Pot plant containers

- Wheels.

- **Squares:**

- Windows

- Dice

- Chocolate squares

- Cakes

- **Rectangles:**

- Doors

- Microwaves

- Windows

- Books

- **Triangles:**

- Pizza slice

- Pyramid

- Your hands can make triangle shapes

- The roof of a house

- **Ovals:**

- Eggs

- Football

- Some mirrors

- Avocado

- **Hexagons (6 sides):**

- Honeycomb / Bee hive

- Bolt

- Floor tiles

- The pattern on a soccer ball

- **Octagons (8 sides):**

- Stop sign

- Floor tiles

- Jewellery

- Clock face

6: Alphabet

Children often love to sing the alphabet song, and this can be a crucial part of learning.

Ways to extend on it can be to ask, "What can you think of that starts with 'A'?" etc.

Ask them to draw. If they suggest an animal you can talk about the sounds they make, or pretend to be one (eg. a rabbit hopping).

Here are a few suggestions of each letter to help get you started:

A: Apple; Aeroplane; Ant

B: Ball; Baby; Blue

C: Cat; Car; Caravan

D: Dog; Duck; Doll

E: Elephant; Egg; Eye

F: Fish; Frog; Fairy

G: Goat; Ghost; Gold

H: Hippopotamus; Hair; Home

I: Ice Cream; Igloo; Iris (coloured part of the eye)

J: Jump; Jeans; Jelly

K: Kangaroo; Koala; Key

L: Love; Lion; Light

M: Man; Moon; Mouse

N: Necklace; Noodles; Newspaper

O: Orange; Opossum; Oven

P: Purple; Princess; Party

Q: Queen; Quail; Quilt

R: Rabbit; Rainbow; Robot

S: Sun; Spaghetti; Soccer

T: Tree; Tiger; Train

U: Umbrella; Unicorn; Ukelele

V: Violin; Volcano; Vegetables

W: Whale; Water; Walrus

X: Xylophone; X-ray; Xenopus (a type of frog)

Y: Yellow; Yoga; Yacht

Z: Zebra; Zucchini; Zip

6: Animals

What colour is it?

What letter does it start with?

How many legs does it have?

What colour / colours is it?

What does it eat?

What letter does that food start with?

Encourage them to draw the animal – in real colours and imaginative ones.

What songs might include this animal?

6: Imaginative Play

Children love to play, and love to play pretend.

Whether they are in the sandpit, climbing trees, building pillow and blanket forts or playing with blocks, there are so many ways to drop in a quick little moment of learning.

The following are only a set of starters to prompt you.

- **In the sandpit:**
  - What colour is the sand?
  - What letter does that start with?
  - How does it feel?

- **Climbing trees:**

- What colour is the tree? leaves?

- What letter does that start with?

- Can you see anything hiding in the tree? (insects, birds etc).

- **Building forts:**

- How many pillows have you used?

- What shape are they?

- What colours are they?

- **Blocks:**

- What are you building?

- What letter does that start with?

- How many blocks have you used?

7: Colours

What is your child's favourite colour? _____

Primary colours are red, blue, and yellow.

Secondary colours are purple, green, and orange.

Red + blue = purple.

Blue + yellow = green.

Yellow + red = orange.

Red + white = pink.

Black is no colour.

White is all colours – *if you have a prism or a crystal you can show how the light breaks up into a rainbow.*

Black + white = grey.

Rainbow colours, in order: Red; Orange; Yellow; Green; Blue; Indigo; Violet

What letter does THEIR FAVOURITE COLOUR _____ start with?

What other things start with that letter?

How many things can you see that start with (the first letter of the favourite colour)?

What COLOUR _____ things do you like to eat?

(If the favourite colour is a **primary colour**):
What colour do you get if you mix
THEIR FAVOURITE COLOUR _____ and ANOTHER COLOUR?

(If the favourite colour is a **secondary colour**):
What colours do you mix to make THEIR FAVOURITE COLOUR _____ ?

Can you think of any songs about THEIR FAVOURITE COLOUR _____ ?

Encourage them to draw things in THEIR FAVOURITE COLOUR.

7: Numbers

For young children, counting should be a reasonably simple task, starting with very basic and working their way up.

How many tummies do you have? *(The answer is one, even if they do seem to eat like they have 2!)*

How many necks?

How many backs?

How many hands do you have?

How many legs / eyes / ears etc?

How many thumbs?

How many fingers? *(It's up to you if you count thumbs along with the fingers)*

This is where you can start to show how different groups can still make the same number (eg. 2 fingers + 2 fingers, or, 3 fingers + 1 finger, or, 4 fingers – all add up to 4).

A song like BINGO is good for learning about the sequence, clapping as each letter of the name is replaced.

There are numerous other songs about counting (I'm *not* thinking of '99 bottles of pop on the wall'!) You can find many examples online to sing along with.

If your child is interested in animals, count how many eyes, legs, different colours etc. they have.

Older children may be able to start to discuss the letters that numbers start with (One is 'o' – even though it sounds like a 'w'; Two is 't' etc).

You can encourage children to draw or write the numbers, draw groups of objects (eg. cars, animals), that have a specific number – one car, two dogs etc.

They may prefer to count physical objects – how many toy cars, how many books, how many cookies (and then you can talk about how many things have been subtracted!)

7: Shapes

Knowing which shapes your child might be interested in can help you be on the look out for them in everyday life.

If they particularly like physical play you can encourage them to make, build or draw different shapes.

Here are a few examples.

- **Circles:**

- Eyes

- Your hand/s can make small and big circle shapes

- Pot plant containers

- Wheels.

- **Squares:**

- Windows

- Dice

- Chocolate squares

- Cakes

- **Rectangles:**

- Doors

- Microwaves

- Windows

- Books

- **Triangles:**

- Pizza slice

- Pyramid

- Your hands can make triangle shapes

- The roof of a house

- **Ovals:**

  - Eggs

  - Football

  - Some mirrors

  - Avocado

- **Hexagons (6 sides):**

  - Honeycomb / Bee hive

  - Bolt

  - Floor tiles

  - The pattern on a soccer ball

- **Octagons (8 sides):**

  - Stop sign

  - Floor tiles

  - Jewellery

  - Clock face

7: Alphabet

Children often love to sing the alphabet song, and this can be a crucial part of learning.

Ways to extend on it can be to ask, "What can you think of that starts with 'A'?" etc.

Ask them to draw. If they suggest an animal you can talk about the sounds they make, or pretend to be one (eg. a rabbit hopping).

Here are a few suggestions of each letter to help get you started:

A: Apple; Aeroplane; Ant

B: Ball; Baby; Blue

C: Cat; Car; Caravan

D: Dog; Duck; Doll

E: Elephant; Egg; Eye

F: Fish; Frog; Fairy

G: Goat; Ghost; Gold

H: Hippopotamus; Hair; Home

I: Ice Cream; Igloo; Iris (coloured part of the eye)

J: Jump; Jeans; Jelly

K: Kangaroo; Koala; Key

L: Love; Lion; Light

M: Man; Moon; Mouse

N: Necklace; Noodles; Newspaper

O: Orange; Opossum; Oven

P: Purple; Princess; Party

Q: Queen; Quail; Quilt

R: Rabbit; Rainbow; Robot

S: Sun; Spaghetti; Soccer

T: Tree; Tiger; Train

U: Umbrella; Unicorn; Ukelele

V: Violin; Volcano; Vegetables

W: Whale; Water; Walrus

X: Xylophone; X-ray; Xenopus (a type of frog)

Y: Yellow; Yoga; Yacht

Z: Zebra; Zucchini; Zip

7: Animals

What colour is it?

What letter does it start with?

How many legs does it have?

What colour / colours is it?

What does it eat?

What letter does that food start with?

Encourage them to draw the animal – in real colours and imaginative ones.

What songs might include this animal?

7: Imaginative Play

Children love to play, and love to play pretend.

Whether they are in the sandpit, climbing trees, building pillow and blanket forts or playing with blocks, there are so many ways to drop in a quick little moment of learning.

The following are only a set of starters to prompt you.

- **In the sandpit:**
  - What colour is the sand?
  - What letter does that start with?
  - How does it feel?

- **Climbing trees:**

  - What colour is the tree? leaves?

  - What letter does that start with?

  - Can you see anything hiding in the tree? (insects, birds etc).

- **Building forts:**

  - How many pillows have you used?

  - What shape are they?

  - What colours are they?

- **Blocks:**

  - What are you building?

  - What letter does that start with?

  - How many blocks have you used?

8: Colours

What is your child's favourite colour? _____

Primary colours are red, blue, and yellow.

Secondary colours are purple, green, and orange.

Red + blue = purple.

Blue + yellow = green.

Yellow + red = orange.

Red + white = pink.

Black is no colour.

White is all colours – *if you have a prism or a crystal you can show how the light breaks up into a rainbow.*

Black + white = grey.

Rainbow colours, in order: Red; Orange; Yellow; Green; Blue; Indigo; Violet

What letter does THEIR FAVOURITE COLOUR _____ start with?

What other things start with that letter?

How many things can you see that start with (the first letter of the favourite colour)?

What COLOUR _____ things do you like to eat?

(If the favourite colour is a **primary colour**):
What colour do you get if you mix
THEIR FAVOURITE COLOUR _____ and ANOTHER COLOUR?

(If the favourite colour is a **secondary colour**):
What colours do you mix to make THEIR FAVOURITE COLOUR _____ ?

Can you think of any songs about THEIR FAVOURITE COLOUR _____ ?

Encourage them to draw things in THEIR FAVOURITE COLOUR.

8: Numbers

For young children, counting should be a reasonably simple task, starting with very basic and working their way up.

How many tummies do you have? *(The answer is one, even if they do seem to eat like they have 2!)*

How many necks?

How many backs?

How many hands do you have?

How many legs / eyes / ears etc?

How many thumbs?

How many fingers? *(It's up to you if you count thumbs along with the fingers)*

This is where you can start to show how different groups can still make the same number (eg. 2 fingers + 2 fingers, or, 3 fingers + 1 finger, or, 4 fingers – all add up to 4).

A song like BINGO is good for learning about the sequence, clapping as each letter of the name is replaced.

There are numerous other songs about counting (I'm *not* thinking of '99 bottles of pop on the wall'!) You can find many examples online to sing along with.

If your child is interested in animals, count how many eyes, legs, different colours etc. they have.

Older children may be able to start to discuss the letters that numbers start with (One is 'o' – even though it sounds like a 'w'; Two is 't' etc).

You can encourage children to draw or write the numbers, draw groups of objects (eg. cars, animals), that have a specific number – one car, two dogs etc.

They may prefer to count physical objects – how many toy cars, how many books, how many cookies (and then you can talk about how many things have been subtracted!)

8: Shapes

Knowing which shapes your child might be interested in can help you be on the look out for them in everyday life.

If they particularly like physical play you can encourage them to make, build or draw different shapes.

Here are a few examples.

- **Circles:**
- Eyes
- Your hand/s can make small and big circle shapes
- Pot plant containers

- Wheels.

- **Squares:**

- Windows

- Dice

- Chocolate squares

- Cakes

- **Rectangles:**

- Doors

- Microwaves

- Windows

- Books

- **Triangles:**

- Pizza slice

- Pyramid

- Your hands can make triangle shapes

- The roof of a house

- **Ovals:**

- Eggs

- Football

- Some mirrors

- Avocado

- **Hexagons (6 sides):**

- Honeycomb / Bee hive

- Bolt

- Floor tiles

- The pattern on a soccer ball

- **Octagons (8 sides):**

- Stop sign

- Floor tiles

- Jewellery

- Clock face

8: Alphabet

Children often love to sing the alphabet song, and this can be a crucial part of learning.

Ways to extend on it can be to ask, "What can you think of that starts with 'A'?" etc.

Ask them to draw. If they suggest an animal you can talk about the sounds they make, or pretend to be one (eg. a rabbit hopping).

Here are a few suggestions of each letter to help get you started:

A: Apple; Aeroplane; Ant

B: Ball; Baby; Blue

C: Cat; Car; Caravan

D: Dog; Duck; Doll

E: Elephant; Egg; Eye

F: Fish; Frog; Fairy

G: Goat; Ghost; Gold

H: Hippopotamus; Hair; Home

I: Ice Cream; Igloo; Iris (coloured part of the eye)

J: Jump; Jeans; Jelly

K: Kangaroo; Koala; Key

L: Love; Lion; Light

M: Man; Moon; Mouse

N: Necklace; Noodles; Newspaper

O: Orange; Opossum; Oven

P: Purple; Princess; Party

Q: Queen; Quail; Quilt

R: Rabbit; Rainbow; Robot

S: Sun; Spaghetti; Soccer

T: Tree; Tiger; Train

U: Umbrella; Unicorn; Ukelele

V: Violin; Volcano; Vegetables

W: Whale; Water; Walrus

X: Xylophone; X-ray; Xenopus (a type of frog)

Y: Yellow; Yoga; Yacht

Z: Zebra; Zucchini; Zip

8: Animals

What colour is it?

What letter does it start with?

How many legs does it have?

What colour / colours is it?

What does it eat?

What letter does that food start with?

Encourage them to draw the animal – in real colours and imaginative ones.

What songs might include this animal?

8: Imaginative Play

Children love to play, and love to play pretend.

Whether they are in the sandpit, climbing trees, building pillow and blanket forts or playing with blocks, there are so many ways to drop in a quick little moment of learning.

The following are only a set of starters to prompt you.

- **In the sandpit:**
- What colour is the sand?
- What letter does that start with?
- How does it feel?

- **Climbing trees:**

- What colour is the tree? leaves?

- What letter does that start with?

- Can you see anything hiding in the tree? (insects, birds etc).

- **Building forts:**

- How many pillows have you used?

- What shape are they?

- What colours are they?

- **Blocks:**

- What are you building?

- What letter does that start with?

- How many blocks have you used?

9: Colours

What is your child's favourite colour? _____

Primary colours are red, blue, and yellow.

Secondary colours are purple, green, and orange.

Red + blue = purple.

Blue + yellow = green.

Yellow + red = orange.

Red + white = pink.

Black is no colour.

White is all colours – *if you have a prism or a crystal you can show how the light breaks up into a rainbow.*

Black + white = grey.

Rainbow colours, in order: Red; Orange; Yellow; Green; Blue; Indigo; Violet

What letter does THEIR FAVOURITE COLOUR _____ start with?

What other things start with that letter?

How many things can you see that start with (the first letter of the favourite colour)?

What COLOUR _____ things do you like to eat?

(If the favourite colour is a **primary colour**):
What colour do you get if you mix
THEIR FAVOURITE COLOUR _____ and ANOTHER COLOUR?

(If the favourite colour is a **secondary colour**):
What colours do you mix to make THEIR FAVOURITE COLOUR _____ ?

Can you think of any songs about THEIR FAVOURITE COLOUR _____ ?

Encourage them to draw things in THEIR FAVOURITE COLOUR.

9: Numbers

For young children, counting should be a reasonably simple task, starting with very basic and working their way up.

How many tummies do you have? *(The answer is one, even if they do seem to eat like they have 2!)*

How many necks?

How many backs?

How many hands do you have?

How many legs / eyes / ears etc?

How many thumbs?

How many fingers? *(It's up to you if you count thumbs along with the fingers)*

This is where you can start to show how different groups can still make the same number (eg. 2 fingers + 2 fingers, or, 3 fingers + 1 finger, or, 4 fingers – all add up to 4).

A song like BINGO is good for learning about the sequence, clapping as each letter of the name is replaced.

There are numerous other songs about counting (I'm *not* thinking of '99 bottles of pop on the wall'!) You can find many examples online to sing along with.

If your child is interested in animals, count how many eyes, legs, different colours etc. they have.

Older children may be able to start to discuss the letters that numbers start with (One is 'o' – even though it sounds like a 'w'; Two is 't' etc).

You can encourage children to draw or write the numbers, draw groups of objects (eg. cars, animals), that have a specific number – one car, two dogs etc.

They may prefer to count physical objects – how many toy cars, how many books, how many cookies (and then you can talk about how many things have been subtracted!)

9: Shapes

Knowing which shapes your child might be interested in can help you be on the look out for them in everyday life.

If they particularly like physical play you can encourage them to make, build or draw different shapes.

Here are a few examples.

- **Circles:**

- Eyes

- Your hand/s can make small and big circle shapes

- Pot plant containers

- Wheels.

- **Squares:**

- Windows

- Dice

- Chocolate squares

- Cakes

- **Rectangles:**

- Doors

- Microwaves

- Windows

- Books

- **Triangles:**

- Pizza slice

- Pyramid

- Your hands can make triangle shapes

- The roof of a house

- **Ovals:**

  - Eggs

  - Football

  - Some mirrors

  - Avocado

- **Hexagons (6 sides):**

  - Honeycomb / Bee hive

  - Bolt

  - Floor tiles

  - The pattern on a soccer ball

- **Octagons (8 sides):**

  - Stop sign

  - Floor tiles

  - Jewellery

  - Clock face

9: Alphabet

Children often love to sing the alphabet song, and this can be a crucial part of learning.

Ways to extend on it can be to ask, "What can you think of that starts with 'A'?" etc.

Ask them to draw. If they suggest an animal you can talk about the sounds they make, or pretend to be one (eg. a rabbit hopping).

Here are a few suggestions of each letter to help get you started:

A: Apple; Aeroplane; Ant

B: Ball; Baby; Blue

C: Cat; Car; Caravan

D: Dog; Duck; Doll

E: Elephant; Egg; Eye

F: Fish; Frog; Fairy

G: Goat; Ghost; Gold

H: Hippopotamus; Hair; Home

I: Ice Cream; Igloo; Iris (coloured part of the eye)

J: Jump; Jeans; Jelly

K: Kangaroo; Koala; Key

L: Love; Lion; Light

M: Man; Moon; Mouse

N: Necklace; Noodles; Newspaper

O: Orange; Opossum; Oven

P: Purple; Princess; Party

Q: Queen; Quail; Quilt

R: Rabbit; Rainbow; Robot

S: Sun; Spaghetti; Soccer

T: Tree; Tiger; Train

U: Umbrella; Unicorn; Ukelele

V: Violin; Volcano; Vegetables

W: Whale; Water; Walrus

X: Xylophone; X-ray; Xenopus (a type of frog)

Y: Yellow; Yoga; Yacht

Z: Zebra; Zucchini; Zip

9: Animals

What colour is it?

What letter does it start with?

How many legs does it have?

What colour / colours is it?

What does it eat?

What letter does that food start with?

Encourage them to draw the animal – in real colours and imaginative ones.

What songs might include this animal?

9: Imaginative Play

Children love to play, and love to play pretend.

Whether they are in the sandpit, climbing trees, building pillow and blanket forts or playing with blocks, there are so many ways to drop in a quick little moment of learning.

The following are only a set of starters to prompt you.

- **In the sandpit:**
  - What colour is the sand?
  - What letter does that start with?
  - How does it feel?

- **Climbing trees:**

- What colour is the tree? leaves?

- What letter does that start with?

- Can you see anything hiding in the tree? (insects, birds etc).

- **Building forts:**

- How many pillows have you used?

- What shape are they?

- What colours are they?

- **Blocks:**

- What are you building?

- What letter does that start with?

- How many blocks have you used?

10: Colours

What is your child's favourite colour? _____

Primary colours are red, blue, and yellow.

Secondary colours are purple, green, and orange.

Red + blue = purple.

Blue + yellow = green.

Yellow + red = orange.

Red + white = pink.

Black is no colour.

White is all colours – *if you have a prism or a crystal you can show how the light breaks up into a rainbow.*

Black + white = grey.

Rainbow colours, in order: Red; Orange; Yellow; Green; Blue; Indigo; Violet

What letter does THEIR FAVOURITE COLOUR _____ start with?

What other things start with that letter?

How many things can you see that start with (the first letter of the favourite colour)?

What COLOUR _____ things do you like to eat?

(If the favourite colour is a **primary colour**):
What colour do you get if you mix
THEIR FAVOURITE COLOUR _____ and ANOTHER COLOUR?

(If the favourite colour is a **secondary colour**):
What colours do you mix to make THEIR FAVOURITE COLOUR _____ ?

Can you think of any songs about THEIR FAVOURITE COLOUR _____ ?

Encourage them to draw things in THEIR FAVOURITE COLOUR.

10: Numbers

For young children, counting should be a reasonably simple task, starting with very basic and working their way up.

How many tummies do you have? *(The answer is one, even if they do seem to eat like they have 2!)*

How many necks?

How many backs?

How many hands do you have?

How many legs / eyes / ears etc?

How many thumbs?

How many fingers? *(It's up to you if you count thumbs along with the fingers)*

This is where you can start to show how different groups can still make the same number (eg. 2 fingers + 2 fingers, or, 3 fingers + 1 finger, or, 4 fingers – all add up to 4).

A song like BINGO is good for learning about the sequence, clapping as each letter of the name is replaced.

There are numerous other songs about counting (I'm *not* thinking of '99 bottles of pop on the wall'!) You can find many examples online to sing along with.

If your child is interested in animals, count how many eyes, legs, different colours etc. they have.

Older children may be able to start to discuss the letters that numbers start with (One is 'o' – even though it sounds like a 'w'; Two is 't' etc).

You can encourage children to draw or write the numbers, draw groups of objects (eg. cars, animals), that have a specific number – one car, two dogs etc.

They may prefer to count physical objects – how many toy cars, how many books, how many cookies (and then you can talk about how many things have been subtracted!)

10: Shapes

Knowing which shapes your child might be interested in can help you be on the look out for them in everyday life.

If they particularly like physical play you can encourage them to make, build or draw different shapes.

Here are a few examples.

- **Circles:**
- Eyes
- Your hand/s can make small and big circle shapes
- Pot plant containers

- Wheels.

- **Squares:**

- Windows

- Dice

- Chocolate squares

- Cakes

- **Rectangles:**

- Doors

- Microwaves

- Windows

- Books

- **Triangles:**

- Pizza slice

- Pyramid

- Your hands can make triangle shapes

- The roof of a house

- **Ovals:**

- Eggs

- Football

- Some mirrors

- Avocado

- **Hexagons (6 sides):**

- Honeycomb / Bee hive

- Bolt

- Floor tiles

- The pattern on a soccer ball

- **Octagons (8 sides):**

- Stop sign

- Floor tiles

- Jewellery

- Clock face

10: Alphabet

Children often love to sing the alphabet song, and this can be a crucial part of learning.

Ways to extend on it can be to ask, "What can you think of that starts with 'A'?" etc.

Ask them to draw. If they suggest an animal you can talk about the sounds they make, or pretend to be one (eg. a rabbit hopping).

Here are a few suggestions of each letter to help get you started:

A: Apple; Aeroplane; Ant

B: Ball; Baby; Blue

C: Cat; Car; Caravan

D: Dog; Duck; Doll

E: Elephant; Egg; Eye

F: Fish; Frog; Fairy

G: Goat; Ghost; Gold

H: Hippopotamus; Hair; Home

I: Ice Cream; Igloo; Iris (coloured part of the eye)

J: Jump; Jeans; Jelly

K: Kangaroo; Koala; Key

L: Love; Lion; Light

M: Man; Moon; Mouse

N: Necklace; Noodles; Newspaper

O: Orange; Opossum; Oven

P: Purple; Princess; Party

Q: Queen; Quail; Quilt

R: Rabbit; Rainbow; Robot

S: Sun; Spaghetti; Soccer

T: Tree; Tiger; Train

U: Umbrella; Unicorn; Ukelele

V: Violin; Volcano; Vegetables

W: Whale; Water; Walrus

X: Xylophone; X-ray; Xenopus (a type of frog)

Y: Yellow; Yoga; Yacht

Z: Zebra; Zucchini; Zip

10: Animals

What colour is it?

What letter does it start with?

How many legs does it have?

What colour / colours is it?

What does it eat?

What letter does that food start with?

Encourage them to draw the animal – in real colours and imaginative ones.

What songs might include this animal?

10: Imaginative Play

Children love to play, and love to play pretend.

Whether they are in the sandpit, climbing trees, building pillow and blanket forts or playing with blocks, there are so many ways to drop in a quick little moment of learning.

The following are only a set of starters to prompt you.

- **In the sandpit:**

  - What colour is the sand?

  - What letter does that start with?

  - How does it feel?

- **Climbing trees:**

  - What colour is the tree? leaves?

  - What letter does that start with?

  - Can you see anything hiding in the tree? (insects, birds etc).

- **Building forts:**

  - How many pillows have you used?

  - What shape are they?

  - What colours are they?

- **Blocks:**

  - What are you building?

  - What letter does that start with?

  - How many blocks have you used?

Also By Matthew Goodall

Te Kōrero o te Moko Kauae – The Story of the Moko Kauae
(bilingual: Māori-English)

I Love You To My Heart

Hickory Hickory Dock – A Counting Rhyme

Wagging His Tail Behind Him

Ka Aroha Au I A Koe Ki Tāku Ngakau
(I Love You To My Heart – Māori)

We All Say Goodnight

The Twelve Days of Christmas

I Wish That I Could Have Ice Cream Every Day

I Te Waokū Pōuriuri – In The Dark Dark Woods
(with Raymond Peeti – bilingual: Māori-English)

About the Author

A disability support worker, and former teacher, Matthew has been reading and writing since before he started school. His first story was mercilessly edited by his parents, and in between fits of laughter, he learned how creative words and descriptions can bring stories to life.

He has a passion for books and sharing stories that will uplift, teach, and transport you to magical places. If you can share a laugh along the way, all the better!

From Aotearoa/New Zealand, he loves weaving in aspects of his home and mythical elements to his stories.

He shares his life with his long-suffering partner, and their Frenchie, Max.

www.ingramcontent.com/pod-product-compliance
Lightning Source LLC
Chambersburg PA
CBHW042115100526
44587CB00025B/4058